When Loss Changes Life

When Loss Changes Life

◆

A Study in Caring

Dr. Charles E. Smith

iUniverse, Inc.
New York Lincoln Shanghai

When Loss Changes Life
A Study in Caring

iUniverse, Inc.

For information address:
iUniverse, Inc.
2021 Pine Lake Road, Suite 100
Lincoln, NE 68512
www.iuniverse.com

ISBN: 0-595-32697-8

Printed in the United States of America

Dedication

This book is dedicated to one whose spirit is as caring as it is gentle and generous. Her name is Norma.

Contents

INTRODUCTION

The writer of Ecclesiastes put time and life into perspective when he said, *"To everything there is a season and a time for every purpose under the heaven."*

—(Ecclesiastes 3:1)

What this ancient writer does is confirm life seldom remains the same for very long and that everyone has the same range of experiences.

In twenty-five years as a licensed Marriage, Family, and Child Counselor, an almost endless parade of individuals came to my office in the wake of experiences of desertion, separation, divorce, and the refusal of responsibility on the part of someone who had helped bring a child into the world.

From them I learned how personal and difficult loss is, how it removes from our lives individuals once present and active, changes the meaning of life, depresses the spirit, generates a host of questions, and forces everyone to decide whether to live in the past and allow life to pass them by, or make a new beginning

◆　　◆　　◆

The focus of this book is caring when loss changes life.

Those who experience loss are challenged to accept loss, encouraged to grieve thoroughly and completely, and cautioned against placing obstacles in their path to adjustment and the restoration of balance to life.

Individuals who respond to those who experience loss are challenged to create an image of themselves as caring persons and become acquainted with concepts of loss and grieving.

Parents in family units formed by loss are challenged to have a healthy grief experience, facilitate the same experience for their children, develop a positive outlook on life, and if children are involved, commit themselves to a post-divorce parenting relationship with a former spouse.

PART I

Challenges Faced by Those Who Respond When Loss Occurs

CHALLENGE NUMBER ONE

TO IMPLEMENT THEIR UNDERSTANDING OF CARING

As the image individuals have of themselves is the window through which they approach others, the image of those who respond when others experience loss must be one in which they see themselves as caring persons.

◆   ◆   ◆

The task of creating a caring frame of reference begins in infancy.

As meaning is built into us, it is well to think of infants as blank sheets upon which those who care for them write in the way they speak, hold, feed, and meet their needs.

When cared for by warm, loving individuals consistent in their caring, infants feel good about themselves and the foundation is laid for a healthy self-image because we feel good about ourselves when our needs are met in warm and loving ways.

On the other hand, when cared for by cold and disinterested individuals whose caring is painful or abusive, infants do not feel good about themselves and the foundation is laid for a negative self-image.

As meaning is built into us, the attitudes of parents and others who care for infants are especially important.

While words are capable of building up or tearing down they are not likely to do permanent damage if the attitudes accompanying them are not judgmental and indifferent.

In the long run what counts is what children live with on a daily basis.

Children who live with acceptance learn to accept others. Those who live with security learn to have faith in themselves, others, and God. Those who live with fairness learn to treat others the way they themselves want to be treated. Those who live with hostility, learn to fight and those who live with criticism learn to judge and condemn.[1]

Infants fortunate enough to be cared for by warm, loving individuals are more likely as adults to feel they have worth and value than are those cared for by individuals who are cold, negative, and indifferent.

◆   ◆   ◆

"Whether it is fortunate or not," writes Edgar N. Jackson, *"it is undoubtedly true that the answers to the basic questions of life are given before the child gains verbal competence.*[2]

As a result of contacts with parents and others who care for them, children arrive at some basic conclusions regarding themselves, others, and the world before celebrating their third birthday.

By age three children have already concluded they are "OK or NOT OKAY," others are "OK or NOT OKAY," and the world is "OK or NOT OKAY" as well.

◆   ◆   ◆

"Okay" and "Not Okay" are ways of seeing oneself, others, and the world.

Seeing oneself as OKAY is believing one has worth and value, is lovable, has something to offer, and is confident of their ability to handle themselves and manage their environment, whereas, seeing oneself as NOT OKAY is feeling one is not lovable, lacks personal worth and value, and has little or nothing to offer.

Regardless of how individuals see themselves, whether OKAY or NOT OKAY in their own eyes, under pressure they will see themselves that way.

If individuals see themselves as OKAY, under pressure they will continue to believe in themselves.

If they see themselves as NOT OKAY, they will doubt their personal worth and value and feel they must do what others want them to do and comply with the demands of others if they are to receive attention.

◆   ◆   ◆

In contemporary society personal worth and value is assessed by comparing people to material things, members of the animal kingdom, and one another.

People are Equal to or of Less Value Than Material Things

Some people assess their personal worth and value by comparing themselves to material things.

In homes where things are more highly valued than people, "No" is a word often heard whenever play, curiosity, or a desire to learn brings children too near a chair, bookcase, lamp, or object considered valuable.

Within limits dictated by safety and due regard for possessions children must have opportunity to explore their world.

In homes where possessions are more valued than people, however, a child's exploration of their world is limited or may never take place, and children learn they are not as important as things.

Little wonder that as adults this unexplored world and people in it seem hostile, threatening, inhospitable, and cold.

People are Equal to or of Less Value Than A Member of the Animal Kingdom

While some individuals assess their personal worth by comparing themselves to material things, others measure their worth by comparing themselves to some member of the animal kingdom.

Proof of this is in the fact that we put food into our stomachs that we would never permit an animal to eat and consume more food than is required for optimal functioning, while we guard the intake of animals as overeating impairs their functioning and diminishes their value.

Furthermore, it's "up and attem" at the crack of dawn to make certain animals get proper exercise while we sometimes become couch potatoes.

Some Men Have More Worth And Value Than Others

In contemporary society the principal method of assessing the worth and value of people is comparing one person to another.

People who are beautiful are favored over those not so beautiful. Those who have good minds (degrees generally accepted as evidence of a good mind) are valued over those who hold no degree. Those whose vocation or accomplishments bring them acclaim and recognition are preferred over those who go about their daily tasks without fanfare or recognition.

Men assess their personal worth by comparing themselves to other men intellectually, while women compare themselves to other women who happen to be taller or shorter, thinner or heavier, whose hair happens to be blonde, brunette, or redhead, as opposed to whatever color their own hair happens to be.

While there is value in comparing oneself to others more often than not it results in someone else becoming the measure of one's life.

If I am to consider myself handsome or beautiful I must look like someone else.

If I am to think myself intelligent I must have similar or better educational preparation than someone else.

If I am to be successful, I must achieve in ways compare favorably to what has made others successful.

◆   ◆   ◆

It would be well to cease assessing the worth and value of people by comparing one to another, for regardless of how beautiful or handsome one may be, how learned one may be (with or without a degree), or what one has done, there is always someone better looking, who has read more, holds more degrees, possesses more innate talent and ability, and has achieved more.

One thing is clear. If the worth and value of people is based on anything other than who they are, it will always be up for grabs, as beauty fades with age, intellectual prowess slackens with time, and achieving becomes increasingly difficult.

Most importantly, however, even if by some miracle one were to acquire the looks of a Robert Redford or Shania Twain, the brilliance of an Einstein or Velakovsky, and their achievements were such as to merit a Nobel Prize, they would still be who they are.

Each Person Is Unique.

There is only one criterion for assessing the personal worth and value of people that makes sense, and that is to accept everyone as unique and glory in that.

If, we were to glory in our uniqueness, then when someone comes along who just

- Happens to be more beautiful or handsome than we view ourselves as being

- Possesses more degrees than we do, or knows more without a degree than we do, or whose

- Achievements bring acclaim and recognition, they are not likely to threaten us because our worth and value is not at stake.

It is the realization that they are unique that frees individuals to stop assessing their worth and value by comparing themselves to others.

Meanwhile, the looks, brains, and achievements of others are appreciated for what they are, namely, as things that make others who they happen to be.

◆   ◆   ◆

Research has identified experiences having a bearing on the formation of the image needed in caring for those who experience loss.

How Parents and Care Providers Feel About Themselves

How parents and those who care for children feel about themselves is important, for if a child perceives Mom and Dad and those who care for them feel good about who they are they are able to affirm their own goodness because, "I'm like them."

The Quality and Expression of Love In the Home

It is essential that children know they are loved.

Was love expressed in your family based on who you were or how you behaved?

Was love ever withheld because you were not "good" by some parental standard?

Feeling Important or Unimportant
As a Family Member

Did you feel important or unimportant in your family?

How did members of your family let you know how they felt about you?

Parents let children know they are important by:

- Accepting each one as a person of worth and value with a combination of traits and characteristics, strengths and weaknesses all their own

- Refusing to compare one child to another, and

- Setting standards for their emotional, physical, and social behavior commensurate with their age and level of maturity

It is important that standards set for children be reasonable and compatible with age and level of maturity, for if children cannot live up to standards set for them, they think themselves unworthy and may even be provoked to wrath.

Parents also let children know they are important by

- Celebrating days important in their lives (birthday, Valentine's Day, Christmas, graduation, etc.), honoring their scholastic and athletic achievements, and

- Teaching them to make decisions and permitting them to learn from the decisions they make.

Were you permitted to make decisions? *"Parents can help children learn to make decisions,"* say Drs. John Clabby and Maurice Elias, *"by providing a firm family structure with clearly defined limits, dealing with children at a developmentally appropriate level, by incorporating decision-making observations into everyday family routines and making lessons in decision-making enjoyable."*[3]

Parents also help children feel important by

- Listening to what they have to say, paying special attention to their attitudes and feelings, and

- Administering discipline and correction in a loving and consistent manner.

Scripture admonishes parents to bring up children in the way they should go (Proverbs 22:6), cautions them against withholding discipline and correction (Proverbs 22:13), and warns them against relating to children in ways that provoke them to wrath (Ephesians 6:4).

For discipline and correction to be effective, the goal of parents must be to nurture children rather than obtain compliance to parental demands.

To be nurturing in disciplining and correcting their children parents must separate who children are (which is a relational issue) from what they do (which is a behavioral issue).

Parents unable to make this distinction are likely to endanger relationship with their children by attacking them or tying the reception of love to "being good."

◆　　◆　　◆

In no way does emphasizing who children are imply parents are to overlook, ignore, or excuse what children do. What children do is right or wrong, good or bad, constructive or destructive, okay or not okay, positive or negative, lawful or unlawful, acceptable or unacceptable by some standard.

It would be unfair, however, to ignore how hard it is to discipline what children do without judging them, and equally unfair not to recognize how difficult it is to love children in spite of what they do.

The most damaging consequence of failing to distinguish between who children are and what they do, however, is that it prompts parents to judge their children and teaches children to judge others.

◆　　◆　　◆

It is easy to fall into the habit of judging.

Let's suppose that tonight you go to one of your favorite restaurants.

As you enter you observe a man sitting alone at a corner table eating a steak and lobster dinner.

What does that scene tell you about that man?"

You could say, "He's a traveling salesman," you might say, "he's rich," "he's hungry," "his wife just threw him out," or "he's divorced." If you are single you might even think say "he's available."

Every response made was a judgment!

Why?

Because all that the scene is capable of telling you is that a man is sitting alone at a corner table eating a steak and lobster dinner.

He may, indeed, be a traveling salesman; however, you have no way of knowing that.

And he could be rich, or lonely. But, again, you don't know.

And there is no basis whatsoever for thinking the man has been tossed out by his wife, as his marital status was never established.

The man in the restaurant might conceivably be a clergyman who has spent the day in one meeting after another, therefore, understandably, delighted to be eating his meal free of the necessity of making conversation.

Neither can it be said with certainty that the man is hungry, although, the fact that he is eating a steak and lobster dinner would suggest as much, and incredible as it may seem, he could be eating a second steak and lobster dinner in order to win a wager made with a colleague earlier in the day.

It is even within the realm of possibility that this particular restaurant is the only one open at this hour and, though highly unlikely, steak and lobster is the only item on the menu still available.

Actually, in responding to the man in the restaurant you identified with him so closely that you put yourself in his place and what you really said was, "If I were sitting alone in a restaurant eating a steak and lobster dinner, I would be (the possibilities being) a traveling salesman, rich, lonely, or tossed out by my wife."

Secondly, you judged him. You said, "Because you are sitting alone eating a steak and lobster dinner, you must be a certain kind of person."

But, you don't know.

Yet, the judgment you made is certain to influence how you relate to the man.

CHALLENGE NUMBER TWO

BECOME A CARING INDIVIDUAL

Out of their experience individuals fashion a habitual way of thinking and feeling about the world, people, and what happens to them.

In the way people approach life and the world they reveal (a) their primary need, (b) their primary fear, (c) the way they recognize and demonstrate love, and (d) within reason, where they can be found in the work world.

Learning to identify how those who experience loss approach life and the world can be immensely helpful in caring for them.

Ways People Approach Life and the World

As a Time and Place of Growth and Development

Some people approach life as a time and the world as a place in which to grow and develop. They feel alive, important, and needed when moving in the direction of wholeness, completeness, and self-mastery.

Fear of stagnation is triggered when they cease growing in these ways.

As a Time and Place to be Liked, Loved, Accepted, and Affirmed

While some people approach life and the world as contexts in which to grow and develop, others approach life as a time and the world a place in which one's need to be liked, loved, accepted, and affirmed can be met.

They feel alive, important, and needed when their needs are met and rejected when they are not.

As a Time and Place of Order, Exactness, and Preciseness

A third group of individuals approach life and the world as a time and place in which meaning comes in exactness, preciseness, and detail.

When everything is in order, things are precisely where they should be, and every detail has been attended to, they feel secure. When things are not this way life is chaos.

As a Place Where it is Important
To Be In Control

A fourth group of people approach life as a time and the world as a place in which meaning comes in being in control.

They feel important when they are in charge. Should control be wrested from them or reside in the hands of others they are likely to withdraw or refuse to be involved altogether.

As a Place Best Left Alone

A fifth group of individuals take an apathetic approach to life and the world. As their need is to be left alone, they fear involvement.

◆   ◆   ◆

In general, people are drawn to areas of work in which their needs can be met and their fears are not likely to be triggered. Having this information is immensely helpful in approaching and caring for those who experience loss.

Those whose need is to be liked, loved, accepted, and affirmed are drawn to professions involving a high level of interaction with people, such as teaching, nursing, and sales.

Those whose need is for order are drawn to vocations in which attention to exactness, preciseness, and attention to detail are valued, such as architecture, engineering, and accounting.

Those whose need is to control enter areas in which control is an asset, such as politics, truck driving, and law enforcement, while those whose approach to the world is apathetic are found in jobs that require as little involvement with people as possible.

CHALLENGE NUMBER THREE

DEMONSTRATE THAT ONE CARES

Connected to men everywhere by the bond of humanity, the primary task of those who respond when others experience loss is to demonstrate they care.

Among the many helpful things that can be done at this time is

- Persuade those who experience loss to make a new beginning rather than park and allow life to pass them by

- Help them accept the changes loss brings

- Recommend that loss be grieved thoroughly and completely, and if one is a single parent that they have a healthy grief experience, facilitate a similar experience for their children, and enter into a post-divorce parenting relationship with their former mate

- Encourage them to maintain the vitality of their lives rather than permit their vision to narrow, their motivation to slacken, or anyone or anything to impede or bring progress toward adjustment and the restoration of balance to a halt, and

- Help them move toward adjustment and the restoration of balance to life by sharing presence with them.

Presence is a manifestation of the human spirit in the lives of people.

Because spirit is energy, the power inherent in the presence of those who respond to loss reduces tension, lessens fear and anxiety, and validates the personal worth and value of those who experience loss at a time when it is normal to question oneself along these lines.

Sharing presence is an act of kindness, compassion, and mercy by which those who respond to loss build and cement relations with those whose ties to emotionally significant persons are severed.

Qualities of Presence

Acceptance: The Acknowledging Quality of Presence

Acceptance is simply acknowledging others as persons of worth and value without asking that anything about them be changed.

Valuing: The Assessing Quality of Presence

Valuing is recognizing that God "...*has placed within man, as part of his created nature, resources which make for wholeness, health, growth, the resolution of conflict, the transformation of instinctive conflict and energy into creative living.*"[4]

Valuing impresses those who experience loss that they are important apart from everyone else, from what they own or possess, where they live, and that those who respond to them value their thoughts, ideas, feelings, experiences, attitudes and behaviors as things that make you them who they are.

Sharing: The Affirming Quality of Presence

Sharing is the attribute of presence by which caregivers bring comfort and assurance to the lives of others.

Commitment: The Cementing Quality of Presence

Commitment is the quality of presence that enables those who respond when loss occurs, to dedicate themselves to meeting the needs and acting in the best interest of those who experience loss.

Intimacy: The Expressive Quality
Of Presence

Intimacy is shared closeness. It is not "*so much a matter of what or how much is shared*" say Howard T. and Charlotte Clinebell, "*as it is the degree to which one's needs are met in a relationship.*"[5]

Lacking closeness individuals feel alone in some way.

Those in society with vested interests believe opportunities for closeness are enhanced by wearing the right clothes, driving the right cars, drinking the right drinks, wearing the right aftershave or cologne, and going to the right places.

Those who respond can inform those who experience loss of avenues available for experiencing closeness, and encourage them to use as many of these avenues as are appropriate, avoiding ones denied them by an absence of commitment or the tenets of their faith.

Avenues of Intimacy

Emotional Intimacy

Emotional intimacy is sharing one's innermost self with others.

The poet Goethe verbalized the possibilities of emotional intimacy when he said, *"If you have one person with whom you can share your innermost being that person will make life a garden for you."*

Intellectual Intimacy

Intellectual intimacy is sharing thoughts and ideas with others and accepting their thoughts and ideas in return though they may differ from one's own.

Aesthetic Intimacy

Aesthetic intimacy is sharing experiences of beauty, art, music, and drama.

In the interest of closeness one individual attends the ballet while another goes to a rodeo.

Creative Intimacy

Creative intimacy is working with others to bring into being something pleasing, aesthetic, or functional.

What that something happens to be is immaterial. What is important is the feeling of closeness that comes in collaboration with others.

Recreational Intimacy

Recreational intimacy is sharing an activity rather than competing with others.

Individuals driven to win might well ask themselves, "Why is it so important that I win or prove myself better or superior to others?"

Whatever the reason, it constitutes a barrier to intimacy.

Work Intimacy

Work intimacy is sharing a task (be it cutting the grass, painting the house, or packing furniture in preparation for a move).

Closeness is experienced in each person carrying their own weight, yet, appreciating the contribution of others.

Crisis Intimacy

Crisis intimacy is focusing on "what can be done" or "what is the best thing to do" as opposed to electing to investigate, blame, and judge.

Experience demonstrates something can be done in most instances. Even when there appears no way of resolving a situation, one can always change their attitude toward the situation and persons involved in it.

Conflict Intimacy

Intimacy in situations of conflict comes as individuals focus on resolving differences before they become unmanageable without needing to be right, prove another wrong, or put another down.

Commitment Intimacy

Intimacy grows as individuals dedicate themselves to meeting the needs and acting in the best interests of others in spite of how they may feel about what others do, say, think, and feel.

Committing oneself to doing "the loving thing" in spite of how one feels, suggests we are most loving in the absence of feelings of love.

Spiritual Intimacy

We experience spiritual closeness by sharing matters of ultimate importance with others (such as salvation, baptism, heaven, eternity, hell, abortion) without requiring them to agree with our position.

Communication Intimacy

Individuals demonstrate a desire for closeness in their willingness to work at clarifying meanings.

Intimacy in communication is tricky simply because people don't always say what they mean and mean what they say, and because "meanings lie in people."

For example, to the owner of a nightclub a "bastard" is an unruly patron who has been ejected. To a historian the word refers to an illegitimate heir to the throne, while to a carpenter, a bastard is a file.

So important is communication to the health of relationships that Father John Powell identifies it as the secret of staying in love.

Sexual Intimacy

Sexual intimacy is the most complete and significant way of experiencing closeness with another person.

Husbands and wives make their desire for intimacy known to their spouse confident their need will be met if possible.

Partners in marriage withhold themselves from each other sexually for health reasons and while performing acts of piety such as fasting and prayer.

Because sexual desire varies with the individual and is influenced by a variety of factors at each stage of life, one's approach to and sexual intimacy changes as life advances.

CHALLENGE NUMBER FOUR

TO UNDERSTAND LOSS AND HOW IT CHANGES THE MEANING OF LIFE

Loss is "anything that substantially changes the meaning of life." It comes to us primarily through death, desertion, separation, divorce, and unaccepted responsibility on the part of someone who helped bring a child into the world.

As loss is personal and subjective to those who experience it, it is imperative that those who respond have an idea of what loss means, become acquainted with the several ways loss changes the meaning of life, and learn as much as possible about the process of grieving, especially, the functions grieving performs.

Ways Loss Changes the Meaning Of Life

Whether voluntary as when men elect to divorce their wives or involuntary as when people are killed in automobile accidents loss

• Throws all areas of life out of balance

• Weakens one's sense of self

• Changes how people feel about themselves

• Revamps one's network of relationships

• Eliminates opportunities for sharing closeness, and if one is a single parent

• Changes the nature of parenting.

Loss Throws All Areas of Life Out of Balance

Loss and the Physical Area of Life

In the wake of loss it is not unusual for some individuals to neglect their personal appearance and physical conditioning while others become super conscious in these areas.

Weight fluctuates up as well as down while grieving, as the appetites of some individuals disappear while others are driven to "pig out" at every opportunity.

Preoccupied with adjusting to the changes loss brings to their lives individuals sometimes fail to take into account that the body is called upon to absorb the pain of loss and that this pain is capable of overloading organs of the body causing them to fail.

Loss and the Thinking Area
Of Life

Loss affects the thinking area of life in a number of ways.

Generally speaking, individuals experience difficulty in concentrating, as the mind tends to flit from subject to subject like a bee gathering honey.

Newspapers lie uncollected on their driveways, magazines are not read, mail goes uncollected, and phone calls are not returned because these things require people to concentrate.

The same page is read over and over. People lock themselves out of home and car, wander endlessly about the house looking for misplaced items, leave electrical appliances unattended, and travel from one location to another unable to recall anything that happened in the interim.

Lacking the ability to concentrate, individuals take the corner off the garage, some have their first automobile accident, and a few lose their jobs.

Loss and the Inner Area of Life

At the core of man's being is an area of spiritual and psychological significance.

Loss affects both dimensions of the inner life. With regard to the spiritual dimension it prompts people to question God, especially, why He didn't intervene and spare them from loss.

And while in some instances the result of this questioning is reduced interest in worship and things spiritual, more often than not it confirms what one believes in ways never before experienced, leading to increased interest in services of worship, bible study, and prayer.

Loss significant affects the psychological dimension of the inner life. It causes people to feel they have changed and to esteem themselves less.

To understand why things are this way understand that

SELF—Is the term by which one person distinguishes himself or herself from everyone else. Self emphasizes one's uniqueness, separateness, and specialness as a person.

Following loss people are less convinced that they have these qualities.

SELF-IMAGE—Refers to the mental picture, idea, or concept that an individual has of themselves in their mind.

Following loss, without being able to explain it, people feel this picture has changed.

SELF-ESTEEM—Is how much an individual likes, loves, accepts, affirms, and takes responsibility for the image they have of themselves.

Following loss people tend to esteem themselves less and feel they are less likeable, less important, and less attractive.

Loss and Relationships

No area of life is affected as much by loss as is the area of relationships.

In general, loss shrinks existing networks of relationships, reduces prospects for social interaction, and narrows the scope of social invitations received.

Explanation for things happening as they do includes recognizing that those who experience loss tend to withdraw temporarily and focus on their own needs.

In addition, couples assume friends who have lost a marital partner would be uncomfortable or feel like a "fifth wheel" at gatherings in which those present are coupled, and out of concern exclude their names from the list of guests invited to parties and other social occasions.

Relationships also change following loss because intelligent, attractive formerly married friends become threats to marriages that are insecure.

Loss Diminishes Opportunities
For Sharing Intimacy

Intimacy is the satisfaction that comes in being close to others. We desire closeness because we are relational beings created with a need to love and be loved, to know and be known by others.

Augustine assessed the human desire for closeness correctly when he observed, *"Our hearts are restless until they find their rest in thee* [God]."

The heart being a symbol of the spirit, what Augustine said of the heart is also true of the spirit. In the same way the heart of man is restless until he finds rest in

God, the spirit of man is restless when ties to others are severed until closeness is experienced in relationship to someone who cares.

In the wake of loss intimacy become something of an issue, as few people are aware of more than one way of experiencing intimacy.

Unaware of other avenues for meeting their need for intimacy, individuals are prone to attempt to meet that need in sexual activity alone.

◆   ◆   ◆

In the wake of World War II, sex, traditionally thought of as a desire or passion was defined as a need.

This redefinition led to an unprecedented upsurge of sexual activity outside of marriage thought of as meeting a need.

Regrettably, nothing was done to inform people of avenues other than sex through which intimacy can be experienced.

As the desire for closeness is strong in those who experience loss, they tend to seek closeness in sexual intercourse.

Attempting to meet one's need for intimacy in sex alone is asking sex to do something it is incapable of doing and was never intended to do, namely, carry the full weight of the human need for intimacy.

Furthermore, as intimacy apart from commitment runs counter to the religious belief of many, those who engaged in sexual intercourse find they had to deal with guilt.

CHALLENGE NUMBER FIVE

UNDERSTAND THE ROLE AND FUNCTIONS OF GRIEVING

Grieving is the process by which individuals mourn their loss, adjust to a world changed by loss, and move toward adjustment and the restoration of balance in life.

To Jill Brooke grieving is the way one reclaims happiness following loss. To Rabbi David Wolpe it is the way we make loss count. For Kenneth Woodward grieving is ritual, while to Lisa Carlson it is the final act of love.[6]

Psychology assures us grieving is normal when loss occurs and that we should expect to grieve because it performs functions that promote adjustment and restore balance to life.

Functions Performed by Grieving
Adaptive Function

The adaptive function performed by grieving helps individuals adjust to the reality that persons once present, active, and available to them are no longer accessible.

Healing Function

The healing function of grieving helps those who experience loss "detach" or "let go" of individuals no longer present and active in life, and cease investing emotional energy in relationships no longer intact.

Social Function

The social function performed by grieving provides time needed by those who experience loss to put every aspect of relationship with individuals no longer available to them into the overall context of their lives.

For some this means performing tasks never before attempted (such as putting gas in the family automobile or doing the laundry), doing things alone that ordinarily were done with another person (such as attending events and services of worship), and building new friendships and acquaintances.

For others it means letting go or rising above experiences, events, situations, and people who contributed to or somehow were involved in one's loss.

◆   ◆   ◆

Grieving and a New Beginning

Making a new beginning is intentionally choosing to change in a desired direction.

Grieving loss thoroughly and completely is essential to a new beginning. Failure to grieve in this way places additional stress upon individuals at a time when they are striving to find meaning, purpose, and direction for their lives, and increases the likelihood that unfinished business and other emotional baggage will be taken into future relationships.

In addition, failure to grieve loss thoroughly and completely clouds the lens of perception causing individuals to confuse "feelings of love" with "being in love," and on that basis to establish emotional relationships before they are ready, or enter relationships in which their needs are not likely to be met.

A Model Grief Process

Thankfully, human beings are created with remarkable capacities for adjusting to loss.

Fortunately we are equipped with what is essentially an emotional defense system that when activated limits the amount of emotional input when ties to emotionally significant persons are severed.

In the book, *Good Grief*, Granger Westberg presents a model grief experience in which individuals pass through a number of stages before adjustment is reached and balance is restored to life.[7]

Shock: First Stage in Grieving

The mood following loss is understandably one of shock as one moment someone emotionally significant is present and active in one's life and the next moment one's tie to that person has been severed.

Essentially, shock is a mechanism intended to defend against additional input by shrinking our emotional world until it is small enough that we feel capable of handling it.

Individuals in a state of shock appear oblivious to surroundings and detached from mundane activities such as reading the newspaper, eating, and doing the laundry.

Emotional Release:
Second Stage in Grieving

Release at this time is rather like having a heavy load lifted from one's shoulders in that it is release from days of endless routine, trips to the hospital, medication schedules, and the necessity of viewing signs of impending loss firsthand.

With emotional release energies previously utilized in keeping one's chin up and maintaining composure are made available to aid in the process of adjustment and the restoration of balance to life.

Isolation: Third Stage in Grieving

To cope with a world changed by loss, individuals tend to withdraw and to one extent or another isolate themselves by ceasing to lead active, visible lives, decreasing contacts with friends, family, and acquaintances, or withdrawing from participation in the Church and service organizations because they are not prepared to handle the emotional climate in settings where numbers of people are present.

Some withdraw because they are uncomfortable over the fact that they failed to deal openly with issues that sapped the vitality of their marriage, and a few withdraw because they need extra time for putting loss into the context of life.

Physical Symptoms of Distress: Fourth Step in Grieving

In general individuals are unaware that feelings generated by loss are absorbed in the body or manifested in some form of bodily distress such as diarrhea, gastric upset, headaches, changes in blood pressure, depth perception, and heart rate.

Also unrecognized is the fact that these feelings can be strong enough to overload organs of the body and cause them to fail.

Guilt: Fifth Step in Grieving

Because loss is a time of review, in many instances guilt is present.

We experience guilt anytime we fail to live up to an accepted standard of values, morality, commitment, and behavior.

Guilt is unhealthy when it hinders healing, when used to avoid responsibility in some way, or when unmerited by one's overall performance in life.

Reflecting on "till death do us part" from their wedding ceremony those who divorce experience pangs of guilt because, while it is the desire of most that their marriage be permanent and indissoluble, some marriages do not last.

Those who may have failed to do everything possible, without surrendering their personhood to create a climate in which reconciliation might have occurred, also experience guilt.

Individuals who hesitated or, perhaps, were negligent in performing some ministration that might have brought relief or made life bearable for someone who was suffering are likely to experience guilt, as are those who recall that in caring for someone over an extended period they became so fatigued that the thought of the death of the sufferer brought a sense of relief.

If, while tending an ailing person there was ever the slightest hesitancy in doing the loving thing, people are likely to experience guilt.

It is unwise to ignore guilt as it can have emotional and spiritual consequences, while dealing with the issue promotes healing and personal growth.

Panic: Sixth Step in Grieving

Panic is the stage in the process of grieving at which loss is felt most keenly.

Unable to focus effectively individuals feel as if they are going to panic. "After all," they reason, "I can't concentrate on anything for very long. I forget things I need to carry out my duties or do my job. I lose my way home. I can't remember my phone number or the numbers of friends. I miss appointments, burn the toast, and boil the coffee pot dry. Are these the actions of a normal person?

Caregivers can assure those who feel they are falling apart that they can make it through this stage of grieving, as panic tends to pass quickly.

Should panic persist, however, it is wise to seek professional help.

Hostility: Seventh Step in Grieving

As people move through the grief experience they become annoyed with themselves unable to perform daily tasks and handle personal matters effectively.

Ordinarily perceived as a negative in daily living, the appearance of hostility suggests individuals have turned the corner and are progressing toward adjustment and balance.

Return to Normal Activities and the Dawning of Hope; Eight Step In Grieving

Hostile at seeing themselves in a negative light and suspecting others see them the same way, those who have been grieving make a tentative return to normal activities.

Hope dawns as loss recedes into the past, new relationships begin filling the void created by the loss of someone emotionally significant, and new, meaningful patterns of participating in life are incorporated into life.

Adjustment and Restoration of Balance to Life: Final Step in Grieving

As grief experiences vary with the individual, "How long should one grieve?"

If as David Viscott suggests "old loves never die, but retreat to a quiet place in our lives," it is important to grieve until individuals emotionally significant to us are in a quiet place in our lives.[8]

If, as Merritt Malloy says, "relationships that have not died peacefully have not died at all," it is essential to grieve until relationships with individuals lost to us have died peacefully in memory, that is, no longer evoke an emotional reaction from us.[9]

To survive the anguish of losing someone emotionally significant to us, we must grieve until as Edna St. Vincent Mallay suggests, we have nothing but good to say of them.[10]

Grieving ends for most people once individuals emotionally significant to them have retreated to a quiet place in their lives and the anguish of death, desertion, separation, divorce, and unaccepted responsibility has been resolved.

CHALLENGE NUMBER SIX

BUILD RELATIONSHIPS WITH THOSE WHO EXPERIENCE LOSS

Over a hundred years ago, Emily Dickinson observed, *"People measure their loss with narrow, probing eyes, wondering if [anyone] understands its weight, or thinks theirs an easy size.*[11]

Take the Initiative

It is well for those responding to individuals who experience loss to take the initiative in building relationships, as going first says someone cares.

Build Trust

To build relationships with those who experience loss those who respond must create an atmosphere of mutual confidence and trust.

Trusting others grows out of trusting oneself. Individuals who trust themselves are able to affirm their strengths, acknowledge their weaknesses, and accept themselves as fragile, faulted, and fallible

Merit the Trust of Others

To merit the trust of those who experience loss those who respond must accept them without reservation.

Acceptance doesn't require that the one who responds like those who experience loss or condone anything they do. It asks only that they acknowledge things that make them the persons they happen to be without making value judgments of any kind or requesting anything be changed.

Acknowledge Factors that Complicate or Make It Difficult To Care for Others

To build relationships in the wake of loss those who respond must acknowledge factors in themselves (personality traits, characteristics, and habits), their experience (disappointment, for instance), and society (prejudices and suppositions) capable of hampering the task of caring.

Maintain Separateness and Self-determination

Building relationships with those who experience loss requires those who respond to remain their own person, separate and self-determining and insist others do the same, for only as they remain separate and self-determining are they able to meet people at the point of need.

Refuse to Introduce Distortion

Those who respond when loss occurs must keep in mind that to facilitate adjustment and help restore balance to the lives of those who experience loss, it is essential to avoid hidden agendas and the temptation to dominate or exercise authority over those who experience loss, view them as sources of physical pleasure and objects of conquest, or see them as persons who somehow do not measure up.

Those Who Respond Must Not Anticipate
Everyone Who Experiences Loss Is Going
To View Them Worthy of Trust

However strong the desire may be to care for those who experience loss, those who respond are not likely to merit the trust of everyone.

When this happens it is wise to be slow to take offence as people who experience loss are fragile, faulted, and frail, and while their imperfections may prevent them from viewing others worthy of trust, it does not excuse those who respond from modeling what is required for one person to trust another.

Recognize the Possibility
Of Hurt, Disappointment, and Loss

It is essential to recognize that responding to those who experience loss opens one to the possibility of hurt, disappointment, and burnout, in part, because the perspective of individuals involved is not the same.

To individuals who experience loss, their situation seems like "the end of the world," or at a minimum, a "grave emergency," while from the perspective of the one responding the situation is one that with wisdom and guidance adjustment and balance can be restored.

Often overlooked is the fact that caring requires tremendous amounts of energy on the part of those who respond, therefore, should these people permit energy in their tank to run low they risk succumbing to "compassion fatigue," the name by which burnout is known among those who care for others.

Recognize Relationships
Have Limitations

There is yet another matter to be considered with regard to responding in situations of loss and that is to recognize that when adjustment has been reached and balance restored to the lives of those who experience loss, relationships end.

PART II

Challenges Faced by Those
Who Experience Loss

THE CHALLENGE OF A NEW BEGINNING

When individuals once present, active, and available to us have retreated to a quiet place in life, loss has been grieved thoroughly and completely, things that cannot be changed have been accepted and those that can be changed have been changed, everyone elects to park or make a new beginning.

It was the Apostle Paul who said, *"Forget what is behind you..."* the experiences, circumstances, events, situations, and happenings which contributed to or have grown out of your loss.

"Strive with your whole being to reach what is ahead"...a richer, fuller, more productive life reached only through determination.

"Run straight toward the goal"...of a new beginning in all areas of life.

As life is continually moving the most realistic, helpful, healthy, and loving thing individuals can do in the wake of loss is make a new beginning.

◆　　　◆　　　◆

Among the several things those who experience loss must do is come to a fresh understanding and appreciation of themselves, affirm life is good, and develop a positive toward life.

◆　　　◆　　　◆

In coming to a fresh understanding of oneself, it helps to visualize the structure of one's life and the several ways loss has changed it.

In some ways a human life resembles the structure of an atom.

Atoms consist of a basic core or nucleus around which electrons orbit.

Take an 8 l/1" x 11" sheet of paper and draw a circle to represent the nucleus of your personal atom.

Inside the nucleus inscribe your name.

Around the nucleus draw a number of smaller circles representing roles that were yours before loss.

If you are male one or more of the following roles might have been yours prior to loss.

- Husband

- Father

- Breadwinner

- Scout leader

- Baseball coach

- Employer

If you are female, one or more of these roles might be yours.

- Wife

- Mother

- Den Mother

- Employee

- Sunday School Teacher

- PTA President

Loss changes the structure of one's personal atom by changing or eliminating one or more roles.

Darken circles representing roles eliminated by loss (such as that of husband or wife).

Loss also increases the importance of some roles (such as parent) because responsibilities associated with them are heavier than before.

Enlarge the circles representing roles that are more important since loss. Shade the enlarged area to represent increased importance and/or responsibility.

While some roles are more important following loss, others are less important because responsibilities associated with them have decreased.

Shade in a segment of circles made less important by loss.

The figure before you is your personal atom after loss.

Shaded areas represent imbalance in one's life. If order and balance is to be restored to the lives of those who experience loss imbalance must be addressed.

In some instances balance will be restored by the renewal or partial renewal of roles eliminated by loss. In other instances, balance can only be restored by the creation of new roles.

CHOOSING A POSITIVE ATTITUDE TOWARD LIFE

Most people visualize their path through life as a straight line.

As loss requires individuals to deviate from the path they had chosen and changes the meaning of life in so many ways, it is essential for those who experience loss to affirm life is good and choose a positive attitude toward it.

Consider the following tool for developing a positive attitude when ties with others are severed.

On an 8 1/2 x 11" sheet of paper, draw a line from one margin to the other. Label this line, "My Path Through Life."

As everyone's Path begins at birth, put your date of birth on your Path near the left margin of the paper.

Your line should look like this—

Illustration No. 1.

My Path Through Life

<u>*Birth*</u>_____

Somewhere near the left margin place an "X" on your Path Through Life to represent the loss you are grieving.

Your Path should look like this—

Illustration No. 2.

My Path Through Life

<u>**Birth**   **"X"**</u>_____

As individuals progress into a world changed by loss they form fresh attitudes toward everyone and everything.

When these attitudes are positive, constructive, helpful, and affirming individuals rise above their Path because they have become more loving.

If, however, the attitudes formed are negative, individuals go below their Path where attitudes are progressively negative, toxic, and destructive.

◆   ◆   ◆

Return to Your Path and write the word "Positive" to right of the "X" above the line and the word "Negative" below and to the right of the "X."

Your line should look like this:

Illustration No. 3

My Path Through Life

<u>**Birth**   **"X" (Positive)**</u>_____
            (Negative)

Return to your Path once more. This time, list the following attitudes in ascending order above and to the right of the label "Positive": Acknowledgement, Acceptance, Appreciation, Approval, Admiration, Adoration, and Unconditional Love.

Your line should now look like this—

<u>Illustration No. 4</u>

Unconditional Love
Adoration
Admiration
Appreciation
Acceptance
Acknowledgement

My Path Through Life

<u>Birth   "X" (Positive)</u>
           (Negative)

The only difference between attitudes above one's Path is the degree of love they represent. The farther one goes above their Path, the more loving attitudes become.

◆   ◆   ◆

Attitudes That Suggest Caring
Acknowledgement

Acknowledgement is the basic level of loving.

Acknowledgement helps to put into perspective the importance of names and why it is important to call people by their name.

As a person's name stands stand for them, remembering their name acknowledges them as persons, affirms them as persons of worth and value, and establishes the fact that someone cares.

Acceptance

Acceptance is at a deeper level of love than that implied by acknowledgement.

It is acknowledging things that make others who they happen to be without permitting these things to alter how one relates.

Appreciation

In a society as aggressive and demanding as the present one, appreciation is a level of love rarely encountered. While we express appreciation for things people do, we seldom express appreciation for people themselves.

Admiration

Admiration is loving people at depths that surpass acknowledgment, acceptance, and appreciation. It is respecting, esteeming, and approving of others for who they are as persons.

Adoration

Adoration is a loftier, more intense level of love than any considered thus far, one usually reserved for God and other revered figures.

Unconditional Love

Unconditional love or agape love is the highest level of love imaginable because it is unconditioned by what people do, have done, or have not done.

◆   ◆   ◆

Return to your Path once more. This time, list the following attitudes in descending order to the right of the label "Negative": Constructive criticism, Criticism, Doubt, Suspicion, Fear, Hate, and Indifference.

Your Path should now look like this:

Illustration No. 6

Unconditional Love
Adoration
Admiration
Appreciation
Acceptance
Acknowledgement

My Path Through Life

<u>Birth   "X" (POSITIVE)</u>
(NEGATIVE)

Constructive Criticism
Criticism
Doubt
Suspicion
Fear
Hate
Indifference

◆   ◆   ◆

Every person, thing, situation, issue, and circumstance in your life is either above or below your Path Through Life in your mind.

Below is a list of people, issues, and circumstances.

• President Bush

• Ex-president Clinton

• Dr. Martin Luther King

• Mother Theresa

• Justice Ruth Ginsberg

• Gay clergymen

- Gay marriages

- Welfare

- Social Security

- An "ex" spouse

Choose an attitude toward each item. If your attitude is positive, put a plus sign (+) beside that item and place it above your Path on the level that corresponds to how you feel.

If your attitude is negative, put a minus sign (-) beside the item and place it below your Path on the level that corresponds to how you feel.

◆   ◆   ◆

Let's suppose your attitude toward Mother Theresa is one of "Admiration" while your attitude toward an ex-spouse is one of "Indifference.

That being the case, take Mother Theresa's name and place it above the line on a level with Admiration and the name of your ex-spouse below the line on a level with Indifference.

◆   ◆   ◆

Why did you put these items where you did? What led you to choose a positive attitude toward Mother Theresa and a negative attitude toward your ex-spouse?

Attitudes toward people tend to be positive when we focus on the bond of humanity we share with them and negative when we focus on what people do or have done.

Nothing said is intended to suggest that what people do or have done should be overlooked or that it is possible to disregard totally what people do.

It's simply that positive attitudes aid the making of a new beginning while negative attitudes hinder movement toward adjustment and restore balance to life.

◆   ◆   ◆

If items below your Path Through Life are there because of the attitude you chose toward them, could you possibly choose to place them somewhere above your Path?

Of course you can! However, it will require that you learn what love is and how to love.

The following definition can help you do this.

"Love is the commitment of my will to meet your needs and act in your best interest in spite of how I feel."

In other words, to change attitudes toward persons, issues, situations, and circumstances that are negative, one must commit their will to meeting their own needs and those of others, and acting in their own best interest and those of others in spite of how one might feel.

No one has a need to think negatively of others or be thought of negatively, do they?

Of course not! Yet, while we are not free from conditions, circumstances, and situations in life, we are free to choose what our attitude is to be toward anything in life.

So, why not elect to take everything and everyone below your Path Through life and by an act of your will put them above it?

It is in your best interest to do so, in part, because it is a fact that you can't be healthy for long is you are not happy, and you can't be happy and harbor negative feelings toward anything in your life.

Secondly, committing yourself to loving everything and everyone in your life is electing to go the second mile, turn the other cheek, and, if necessary, forgive those who somehow figured in your experience of loss.

CHALLENGE NUMBER THREE

REFUSE TO PLACE ROADBLOCKS IN ONE'S PATH OF ADJUSTMENT AND THE RESTORATION OF BALANCE

When loss occurs, especially, when ties to emotionally significant persons are severed, those who experience loss sometimes impede progress toward adjustment and the restoration of balance to life by placing roadblocks in their path.

Roadblocks Placed by Widows

Moving On Is Showing Disrespect

Among the roadblocks widows place in their path is the idea that moving on with life is showing disrespect to a deceased spouse and the marital relationship.

Those who view moving on in this way complicate and prolong the grief process and miss out on opportunities for personal growth, adventure, and new relationships.

Idealizing a Deceased Spouse

Idealizing a deceased spouse is another roadblock widows place in their path.

While loving someone deeply is both positive and good, and thinking highly of another person in spite of any faults or imperfections they might have had is admirable, idealizing a deceased husband or wife does nothing to facilitate forward movement in life or improve the quality of life for a surviving spouse.

Widows often idealize a former marital partner in conversation with others to discourage anyone new from becoming interested in them.

While electing to live out one's life without a marital partner is a choice, being dishonest about one's motivation is unhealthy and self-defeating.

Roadblocks Placed by Those Who Are Deserted

Pretending A Spouse Has Just Gone Away

Among the roadblocks those who are deserted place in their path is one of pretending that someone has just "gone away," but will return.

As desertion is a deliberate act and those who desert seldom return, to pretend otherwise is certain to create problems as in the end, truth, however painful, is easier to live with than false hope or a lie.

Roadblocks Placed by Those Who Separate

When loss is experienced through separation, some individuals pretend nothing has happened.

Separation is a state laden with unforeseen difficulties.

To begin, the status of those who separate is uncertain, as there is no appropriate way of referring to someone who technically is a "we," but for all practically purposes is an "I."

Secondly, as contact between spouses who are separated tends to be sporadic and communication somewhat tentative, should separation continue the tendency is for marital partners to build a world of their own where they are and invest their time and energy in that world, replacing the routines and rituals of marriage with ones appropriate to life as a single adult, and creating a network of support in lieu of the support ordinarily provided by a spouse.

Living in separate worlds, dreaming individual dreams, and setting individual goals increases the possibility that one or both spouses will become emotionally and/or sexually involved with someone before a decision regarding the disposition of the marriage is made.

◆   ◆   ◆

Emotional involvement complicates the lives of separated spouses as it encourages the comparing of a spouse (with whom one is at odds) with someone toward whom one has essentially a courting attitude, no relational conflict has as yet been experienced, and toward whom commitment is limited.

And when, as often happens, one spouse becomes convinced additional effort might result in reconciliation, the emotionally involved spouse must decide where his/her commitment lies and how best to terminate relationship with a third party.

Whether or not reconciliation is possible, it seems unwise to become involved emotionally with someone new until one has completed a thorough grief experience and settled the several personal issues stemming from a broken relationship.

◆   ◆   ◆

If you are considering separation, before taking that step

- Think through your situation carefully. If there is a problem in your marital relationship, it is questionable whether it will be resolved or substantially ameliorated by separation.

  Whatever the problem happens to be, it developed in the marital setting, and in a majority of instances, that is where resolving existing differences or the decision to terminate a marriage is best made.

- Consider it wise to terminate an existing relationship before becoming emotionally involved in a new one, as it is difficult to live in two worlds.

- Recognize that while reconciliation requires much of each person, as long as marital partners feel the bond of their union and reconciliation can be accomplished without either partner surrendering their personhood, and both are willing to commit themselves to a counseling relationship until their differences are resolved or a decision to terminate the marriage is made, it seems wise to work toward reconciliation.

- Consider professional help. Professionals can help clarify situations, resolve long-standing differences, and identify real as well as hidden issues in a relationship.

- Should you decide reconciliation is not possible (there being no commitment to each other or the relationship), terminate the marriage quickly, proceed through a healthy, thorough grief experience, and blessed with wisdom that comes from having honestly and responsibly dealt with one of life's most difficult experiences, launch a new beginning.

PART III
Challenges Faced by Church

Social forces unleashed in the wake of World War II continue to transform society, reweaving its fabric of society, restructuring its institutions, stretching its people to the limits of their flexibility, and altering the system of values that for so long has served as guidelines for behavior.

Caught up in an avalanche of change, Americans began questioning the relevance and value of marriage and the family, weaken their commitment to these institutions, and experiment with marriage-like alternatives such as "living together."

◆　　　◆　　　◆

Considered beneficial to individuals and wholesome in their influence upon society, marriage and family play a decisive role in shaping the personality and character of a nation.

In them we receive our first expression and understanding of love, and children are conceived and nurtured to adulthood.

Through them we perpetuate our democratic way of life and teach our system of religious, social, and ethical values.

In the context of marriage and family we experience the deepest levels of emotional satisfaction and have the most meaningful and fulfilling experiences known to man.

◆　　　◆　　　◆

Robert Weiss drew attention several years ago to changes taking place in areas of marriage and family by noting that Americans were in the process of de-sacrilizing marriage, that is, moving from the idea of marriage as a sacred and holy calling with responsibility to self, society, and God, to a consideration of marriage as a vehicle for realizing individual gratification and an avenue for pursuing happiness.[12]

◆   ◆   ◆

As the Church is dedicated to upholding God's intent for marriage, when marriages terminate in death, desertion, separation, divorce, and individuals refuse responsibility for children they helped bring into the world, the level of its concern is increased.

Though dedicated to upholding God's ideal and intent for marriage, the Church also understands marriages fail and when they do that it has a responsibility to care for those who have experienced loss.

As death, desertion, separation, and divorce present the Church with some of its greatest challenges, what can the Church do to demonstrate that it cares for those who experience loss?

The Church can demonstrate it cares by

- Acknowledging its responsibility to minister to all who experience loss by accepting them, creating opportunities for them to use their gifts in the service of the Church, and preparing those who elect to enter another marriage

- Encouraging the participation and involvement of families created by loss in services of worship, refusing to exclude, segregate, or disqualify them from service and positions of leadership because they have experienced divorce.

- Structuring services of worship that encourage belonging, promote understanding, and increase the well being of those whose lives have been changed in experiences of loss

- Helping single parents create a positive, effective, growth-producing lifestyle, and assist in the parenting of their children

- Affirming that desertion, separation, and divorce does not mar the image of God in humankind, and that

- Debating the rightness or wrongness of divorce accomplishes nothing except create an atmosphere of distrust, and dissipate energies, resources, and personnel needed for ministering to the needs of people.

◆   ◆   ◆

The difficulty with the experience of divorce, however, is that it is charged with emotion. No human experience seems as capable of bringing out the best and the worse in humans as divorce, none more capable of generating intense feelings and eliciting extreme behaviors than divorce.

Yet, while the situation is changing, one still encounters individuals in the Church who feel they have nothing in common with those who divorce.

Generally, those who take this view are not ready to accept those who divorce until they have probed for sin in their lives.

To probe for sin in the lives of people torn by the sundering of the bond of marriage is a remarkably insensitive thing to do.

It forfeits the comfort promised in the Second Beatitude and does nothing to help people find meaning in their experience, as what individuals need when ties to someone as emotionally significant as a husband or wife are severed is to be blessed with the presence of someone whose purpose is to bring comfort and assurance.

In the end, however, the issue is not that sin is or is not present in the lives of those who divorce, but whether followers of Christ are willing to come alongside and share the comfort and assurance of their presence with those who have experienced one of life's most difficult experiences.

◆   ◆   ◆

As one would anticipate, when faced with moral, relational, and spiritual issues having a bearing upon individual and corporate living followers of Christ turn to the Scriptures for guidance.

What they discover with regard to divorce, however, is that Scripture does not contain anything approaching an exhaustive treatment of the subject.

◆   ◆   ◆

The attitude toward divorce in the Old Testament is permissive. The law simply acknowledged divorce as a concession to the hardness of the human heart, a compromise between the ideal and intent of God for marriage and the reality that fragile and faulted people often prove unable to maintain that ideal.

Jesus' teachings on the subject of divorce are recorded in the Synoptic Gospels of the New Testament.

It is well to recall that everything Jesus had to say about divorce was said within the framework of Jewish culture, tradition, and law in which the right to divorce was never questioned.

The rabbis did not debate the right to divorce. Their concern was on what grounds was the right to divorce to be exercised.

"Is it lawful for a man to put away his wife for every cause?" ask the Pharisees in Matthew 19:3.

Emphasizing words found in Deuteronomy 24:1, *"If then she finds no favor in his eyes,"* the School of Hillel taught a man had the right to divorce his wife *"for any cause,"* however trivial.

Underscoring the words, *"that she find no favor in his eyes, because he hath found some uncleanness in her,"* (KJV), the School of Shammai said a man could divorce his wife only on grounds of unchastity, uncleanness, or unfaithfulness.

Jesus does not answer the question. He counters by asking, "Have *you not read that at the beginning the Creator made them male and female, and said, 'For this reason a man will leave his father and mother, and be united with (NIV)* or *(cleave to) his wife, and the two will become one flesh?'"* (Matthew 19:7)

"Why then," they respond, *"did Moses then command a man to give his wife a certificate of divorce and send her away?" (Matthew 19:7 NIV)*

Presumably, the Pharisees anticipated Jesus would both confirm the indissolubility of marriage and reject divorce.

That being the case (and, if as Mark suggests, the intent of the Pharisees was to "tempt" or "test" Him), they were prepared to use his answer against him as divorce was a delicate matter in the area governed by Herod Antipas (where Jesus happened to be), as Herod had been severely reprimanded by John the Baptist for divorcing his wife and marrying the wife of his brother, for which he had been beheaded.

Refusing to be drawn into controversy, Jesus calls the rabbis back to the purpose of God in creating the institution of marriage, reminding them, *"For this reason* [the establishing of a marital relationship] *will a man leave his father and mother, and be united with (cleave unto KJV) his wife: and they will become one flesh."* (Genesis 2:24)

The Hebrew word translated "cleave," "joined," or "united" suggests the bond created by the coming together of a man and woman in marriage is comparable to the bond formed when two pieces of paper are glued together, namely, they become one.

This analogy helps explain why divorce is such a painful experience, for when one attempts to separate two pieces of paper that have been glued together, both are torn.

◆   ◆   ◆

Minimum treatment of divorce in Scripture has resulted in a number of simplistic "black and white" approaches to the issue of divorce and those who divorce in which (a) sin is understood as the only cause for divorce, (b) individuals who divorce and marry again are considered living in adultery, and (c) marriages are to be retained "in law" though they may have terminated "in fact."

While dedication to marriage is commendable and the desire to maintain marital relationships is both right and good, the fact remains that when spouses no longer feel the bond of their union, their marriage has "in fact" terminated.

To retain marriages "in law" that have terminated in fact ignores reality and invites difficulty, for when the distance between spouses is great enough that they no longer feel the bond of their union there is no goodwill on which to build. To retain these marriages in law is ultimately destructive to persons involved.

While insisting that marital relationships be retained in law out of loyalty to a legalistic no divorce ethic may sooth the consciences of some and convince others of their righteousness, it does nothing redemptive for the individuals involved.

Rather than insist marriages terminated in fact be retained in law, why not accept that, whereas, God would not have it so, marriages die, and when they do, the most realistic and merciful, redemptive and understanding, loving and compassionate thing the Church can do is encourage individuals to follow the counsel of the Apostle Paul and seek the way that promotes peace.

Marital partners who have struggled with each other, yet, still sense the bond of their union, may find peace in separation and/or reconciliation.

Regrettably, however, regardless of how sincere individuals are in their attempts at reconciling their differences, the struggle sometimes becomes so painful that the personhood and emotional balance of those involved are at risk and release must be sought if each person is to survive emotionally and find peace.

Even among those who desire to honor God, there comes a time when the most honest, healthy, and loving thing to do is to terminate marital unions that have become conflicted, trying, and debilitating if integrity, balance, and peace are to be restored to life.

◆   ◆   ◆

THINGS TO CONSIDER BEFORE ENTERING ANOTHER MARRIAGE.

It seems unwise to enter marriage again until prospective partners

- Are convinced they are called to marriage as the state in which their contribution to life, society, country, and God can best be made

- Have received forgiveness for any contribution they may have made to their marital relationship being less effective than it needed to be

- Have grieved their loss sufficiently to insure the amount of unfinished business and emotional baggage likely to be taken into another marriage is minimal

- Have taken into account spiritual, cultural, and social factors having a bearing on the marriage they propose to enter.

In addition, it seems unwise to enter another marriage until prospective partners

- Have decided whether to live in "my" house, "your" home, or "our house"

- Have discussed matters of lifestyle and career, specifically, if a change in lifestyle seems advisable are they prepared to make that change, and should it be necessary to decide whose career is the most important to the success of the marriage, whose that will be

- It seems advisable as well not to enter another marriage until prospective partners have

- Have ascertained the physical health of both persons. If there are questions in this area, each person should have a thorough physical examination and share the findings with the other

- Discussed financial matters, especially, in instances where alimony and/or child support responsibilities are involved, and those in which a pre-nuptial agreement may be required to safeguard assets set aside for children of one or both partners

- Agreed what their relationship to a former partner in marriage is to be, and whether they are willing to form a parenting partnership with that person[13]

- Identified potential problem areas in the relationship they are about to enter, and

- Discussed the kind of ceremony they will have.

While ceremonies for first marriages usually take place in the Church, a smaller, more intimate setting is often chosen when entering marriage again.

In addition, as customs pertaining to first marriages differ from those appropriate for subsequent marriages, attention to such things is needed if all is to go well.

◆   ◆   ◆

The Church might also consider that as virtually all of life's truly significant experiences are ritualized in ceremony, there is value to ending marriages in a Ceremony of Closure.

Members of the helping professions (clergy, counselors, psychologists, psychiatrists, and social workers) are finding a Ceremony of Closure helps

- Facilitate the transition from the marital to the single state

- Former marital partners accept the finality of divorce and put to rest fantasies of reuniting

- Former marital partners to let go or detach from one another, relinquish dreams they had for the marriage, free themselves from bitterness, and make the changes required to launch a new beginning

- Couples acknowledge their contribution to the ineffectiveness of a marriage

- Children accept what it means to "end a relationship"

- Couples affirm that while they have ceased to be husband and wife, they have not ceased to be parents; therefore, it is in their best interest and that of their children that they form a parenting relationship.[14]

◆   ◆   ◆

A CEREMONY OF BLESSING AND SUPPORT

In addition to other benefits provided by a ceremony of closure, a ceremony of this kind would provide the Church an opportunity to pledge its support and pronounce a blessing upon those who divorce.

"As a community of God's people, we acknowledge that even saintly, godly, mature persons fall short of God's ideal and intent in marriage.

Be that as it may, we believe it important to accept responsibility for any contribution one may have made to a marriage being less effective than it might have been.

Secondly, it seems essential that you separate from your former mate as peacefully and completely as possible.

"Let go" of that person. Permit him or her to go out of your life, to be separate from you. Care enough for that person (and yourself) to resist the temptation to hold on to him or her, for to do so is to live in the past and complicate the process of adjustment and the restoring of balance to life.

Let the person once emotionally significant to you retreat to a quiet place in your life.

We acknowledge that as we are as fragile, faulted, and fallible as you, be assured that you have our support, interest, and love as you move forward in life.

In the days ahead, we are dedicated to maintaining your spiritual, psychological, physical, and relational well-being."

A CEREMONY SYMBOLICALLY ENDING MARRIAGE

A Ceremony of Closure would also provide divorcing couples an opportunity to symbolically end their marriage, perhaps, by

- transferring the wedding ring from the left to the right hand or returning the ring to the person who gave it

- extinguishing the flame of the unity candle, and

- giving the bridal bouquet to the presiding clergyman with instructions to dispose of it.

Finally, a Ceremony of Closure would give an opportunity for everyone to pronounce a blessing upon the divorcing couple like the one below.

A Blessing for the Ending of a Marriage

"We come into the world alone, and alone we will depart. As you go your separate ways be assured that the One who has promised never to leave or forsake us goes with you and will be with you to the end of the world.

"As you are once again alone, we pray for renewal and a purifying and deepening of relationship to the one upon whom we all rely for healing and guidance.

"We give thanks for the growth experienced in marriage and pray that the pain that comes from having severed that bond will transform you into a person of compassion, understanding, and love, that in the midst of your aloneness, you may find peace.

Know that God is greater than your pain and more powerful than your feelings, that He will lead you like a shepherd and gather you in His arms and show you mercy.

Place upon the altar of experience the marriage that has ended and pray God will accept all that is lost, but envision all that has been gained.

Place your fears on the altar that you may experience the love that casts out fear.

Place your emptiness on the altar that God may fill you with His love.

Place your hope on the altar that meaning, purpose, and direction will be yours.

Dedicate yourself to becoming whole, whatever the cost, through Jesus Christ, our Lord.   Amen.

Epilogue

Because life does not remain the same for very long and everyone has the same range of human experience, everyone experiences loss.

Those who respond when others experience loss do so because like the Samaritan in Luke's Parable, they see themselves connected to them by the bond of humanity.

To love those whose lives are changed by loss, those who respond must have a vision of what it means to care, see themselves as loving persons eager to implement that vision by sharing presence with those whose ties to others have been severed.

To care means encouraging those who experience loss to make a new beginning, develop a positive attitude toward life, and forego placing roadblocks in their path to adjustment and the restoration of balance to life.

◆   ◆   ◆

When all is said and done, as the range of experience is the same for those who experience loss as those who respond to them, everyone can acknowledge that at one time or another they too, will need the comfort and assurance of someone who cares.

Footnotes

1. Dorothy Law Nolte, *With What Is Your Child Living?* New York: Workman Press, 1998, pp. *Vi-vii.*

2. Edgar N. Jackson, *Understanding Grief (Nashville: Abingdon Press, 1957), p. 36.*

3. John Clabby and Maurice Elias, *Teach Your Children Decision-Making* (Garden City, New York: Doubleday, 1985);Maurice Elias and John Clabby, "How to Teach Decision-Making to Kids," *U.S. News & World Report,* 100:64, April 21, 1986.

4. Carol A. Wise, *Pastoral Psychology* (New York: Jason Aronson, 1980), p. 34.

5. Howard T. Clinebell and Charlotte H. Clinebell, *The Intimate Marriage* (New York: Harper & Row, Publishers, 1966), pp. 28-39.

6. Kenneth L. Woodward, *The Ritual Solution,* Newsweek, September 22, 1997, p. 62; David Wolpe, *Making Loss Matter* (New York: Riverhead Books, 1999); Jill Brooke, *Don't Let Death Ruin Your Life* (New York: Penguin Books, 2001); Lisa Carlson, *Caring for the Dead: Your Final Act of Love* (Upper Access: n.p.), n.p., 1998.

7. Granger Westberg, *Good Grief* (Philadelphia: Fortress Press), 1972.

8. David Viscott, *How To Live With Another Person.* New York: Pocket Books, 1974, p. 38.

9. Merrit Malloy, *Things I Meant to Say To You When We Were Old.* Garden City, New York: Doubleday & Company, Inc., 1977, p. 3.

10. Edna St. Vincent Mallay, *Collected Poems.* (New York: Harper and Row, Publishers, 1956), p. 676.

11. Thomas H. Johnson (ed.), *The Complete Poems of Emily Dickinson* (Boston: Little, Brown and Company, 1960), pp. 272-73.

12. Robert S. Weiss, *Marital Separation. (New York: Basic Books, Inc., Publishers, 1975), p. 8.*

13. Guidelines for conducting the business of parenting are included in Appendix One.

14. The author acknowledges that he did not create the Ceremony of Closure and the blessing that follows. Both came to the author through a friend. They came unsigned, and other than a reference to a priest officiating in the ceremony there was no way of identifying the person who wrote it or the original source and date of publication.

Bibliography

Brook, Jill Brooke. *Don't Let Death Ruin Your Life*. New York: Penguin Books, 2001.

Carlson, Jill. Caring for the Dead: Your Final Act of Love. Upper Access: 1998.

Clabby, John, and Maurice Elias. Teach Your Children Decision-Making. New York:Doubleday, 1985.

Clinebell, Howard J., and Charlotte. H. Clinebell. *The Intimate Marriage*. New York: Harper & Row, Publishers, 1966.

Elias, Maurice, and John Clabby. "How to Teach Decision-Making to Kids," *U.S. News & World Report,* 100:64 (April 21, 1986).

Jackson, Edward N. *Understanding Grief.* Nashville: Abingdon Press, 1957.

Johnson, Thomas H. (ed.). *The Complete Poems of Emily Dickinson. Boston: Little, Brown and Company, 1960.*

Mallay, Edna St. Vincent. *Collected Poems*. New York: Harper and Row, Publishers, 1956.

Malloy, Merit. *Things I Meant to Say to You When We Were Old.* New York: Doubleday & Company, Inc., 1977.

Nolte, Dorothy Law. *With What Is Your Child Living?*

Otto, Herbert A. (ed). The Family In Search of a Future: Alternatives for Moderns. New York: Appleton-Century-Crofts, 1970.

Powell, John. *Fully Human, Fully Alive* (Niles, Illinois: Argus Publications, 1976).

Powell, John. *Why Am I Afraid To Tell You Who I Am?* Niles, Illinois: Argus Communications, 1969.

Powell, John. *The Secret Of Staying In Love*. Niles, Illinois: Argus Communications, 1974.

Toffler, Alvin. *Future Shock* (New York: Bantam Books, 1970

Viscott David. *How To Live With Another Person. New York: Pocket Books, 1974, p. 38.*

Weiss, Robert S. Marital Separation. *New York: Basic Books, Inc., Publishers, 1975.*

Westberg, Granger. *Good Grief* (Philadelphia: Fortress Press, 1972).

Whitman, Harriet Lee. "Guidelines For A Successful Partnership For Post Divorce Parenting, " *Marriage and Divorce Today,* September, 20, 1982, pp. 3-4.

Wise, Carol. Pastoral Psychology. New York: Jason Aronson, 1980.

Wolpe, David. *Making Loss Matter* (New York: Riverhead Books, 1999.

Woodward, Kenneth L. The Ritual Solution, Newsweek, September 22, 1997, p. 62;

Recommended Reading

Clabby, John, and Maurice Elias, How To Teach Decision-Making To Kids," *U.S. News and World Report* 100:64 (April21, 1986).

Smith, Charles E. *New Beginnings For Single-Parent Families*. Poplar Bluff, Missouri: n.p., 1991.

Smith, Charles E. *Loss Changes Life*. Poplar Bluff, Missouri:

Smith, Charles E. *Growing Gold Through Grief*. Poplar Bluff, Missouri: n.p., 2001.

These resources were prepared for inclusion in packets distributed to participants in an after-care seminar titled, *Growing Gold Through Grief*. Available from author at: drcharlessmith@mycitycable.com

For information on seminars conducted by Dr. Smith also available at drcharlessmith@mycitycable.com

APPENDIX

One of the ironies of life is that while one may cease to be husband or wife one never ceases to be a parent, and though no longer married to each other parents must find ways of cooperating in the parenting of their children.

Experience has demonstrated the wisdom of creating a parenting partnership for the purpose of conducting the business of parenting.

GUIDELINES FOR CONDUCTING THE BUSINESS OF PARENTING

Contact between parenting partners must be polite and businesslike. Neither is to use bad language or engage in name-calling as behavior of this kind makes it difficult to conduct business.

As both parents are important to children each is to respect, preserve, and encourage relationship between their children and a former mate and work to insure that children have unimpeded access to that person.

Arrangements involving the children are the responsibility of adults. Children must not be asked to conduct business.

As decision-making is the responsibility of both parents, unilateral decisions are to be avoided.

To determine the best solution each parent is to consult the other (and the children).

Except for emergencies, appointments for conducting the business of parenting are to be made by phone during business hours. Should the timing of a call be inconvenient, parents are to agree upon a time convenient for discussing matters relating to their children.

To insure good experiences for their children agreements made by parenting partners must be clear, explicit, and confirmed in writing. Parenting partners are responsible for keeping all agreements, appointments, and promises made.

If either is unable to keep their word, they are to inform the other and give an explanation.

Parenting partners are not to discuss the children while intoxicated or on drugs. If either attempts to do so the contact should be terminated immediately and rescheduled.

Neither parent is to question the motives of the other, judge their behavior, or assume anything based on past history without checking it out.

Each partner is to give the other benefit of the doubt just as they would if that person were a total stranger.

Neither parent should anticipate nor expect approval from the other as neither is there to have their personal and emotional needs met or to meet the needs of the other person.

Neither person is to insist on what does not work or commit himself (or herself) to something that will not work.

To cultivate good will in the parenting relationship each partner must decide what they are willing to do for the happiness and success of their children.

◆   ◆   ◆

A Prayer for the Ending of a Marriage

"Alone we come into the world, and alone we will depart. In our passage we are assured of the companionship of the One who said 'I will never leave you nor forsake you. I am with you even to the end of the world.'

As I am once again alone, I pray for renewal and a purifying and deepening of my relationship to the one upon whom I am rely for healing and guidance.

I give thanks for the growth I have experienced. I ask that the pain that has come from the severing of the bond of marriage be transformed into compassion, understanding, and love, that in the midst of loneliness, I may find peace.

Acknowledging that all men run with feet of clay, I pray for that I may be forgiven and forgiving as I release my marital partner, and that I might experience healing, knowing that the journey to healing runs through pain.

I know God is greater than my pain and more powerful than my feelings, that He will lead me like a shepherd and gather me in His arms.

I offer now upon the altar of experience the marriage that is now ended.

The sacrifice I bring is myself, my expectations, some of which are not to be fulfilled.

I bring my fears, which often separate me from you and sometimes from my neighbor.

I bring my hopes, which require your direction and purification.

I bring my emptiness, which you alone have promised to fill.

Bring me to wholeness, whatever the cost, through Jesus Christ, our Lord. Amen

0-595-32697-8

Printed in the United States
57616LVS00005B/370-414